EISENHOWER PUBLIC LIBRARY

W9-BPM-559

EISENHOWER PUBLIC
LIBRARY DISTRICT
4652 N. OLCOTT
DEMCO
HARWOOD HTS., IL. 60656

by Mark Stewart

ACKNOWLEDGMENTS
The editors wish to thank Steve Young for his cooperation in preparing this book.
Thanks also to Integrated Sports International for their assistance.

PHOTO CREDITS
All photos courtesy Rob Tringali, Jr./Sports Chrome except the following:

Steve Young - 4 top left, 4 center right, 9, 10, 11, 12, 13, 18, 22 bottom left,
22 bottom right, 23 top left, 46 top
Brigham Young University - 15, 16 left, 22 top, 24 right, 38 top
AP/Wide World Photos - 19, 26 top, 31

STAFF
Project Coordinator: John Sammis, Cronopio Publishing
Series Design Concept: The Sloan Group
Design and Electronic Page Makeup: Jaffe Enterprises, and
Digital Communications Services, Inc.

LIBRARY OF CONGRESS CATALOGING-IN-PUBLICATION DATA
Stewart, Mark.
Steve Young / by Mark Stewart
p. cm. - (Grolier all-pro biographies)
Includes index.
Summary: Covers the personal life and football career of the quarterback who was named Most Valuable Player in Superbowl XXIX in 1995.
ISBN 0-516-20146-8 (lib. binding)–ISBN 0-516-26011-1 (pbk.)
1. Young, Steve, 1961- –Juvenile literature. 2. Football players–United States–Biography–Juvenile literature. (1. Young, Steve, 1961- . 2. Football players.) I. Title. II. Series.
GV939.Y69S84 1996
796.332'092-dc20
(B) 96-5108
CIP
AC

The Grolier All-Pro Biographies™ are produced in cooperation with
Sports Media, Incorporated, New York, NY.

Published simultaneously in Canada. Printed in the United States of America.
1 2 3 4 5 6 7 8 9 10 R 05 04 03 02 01 00 99 98 97 96

Grolier ALL-PRO Biographies™

Steve Young

by

Mark Stewart

CHILDREN'S PRESS®
A Division of Grolier Publishing
New York • London • Hong Kong • Sydney
Danbury, Connecticut

Contents

Who

Am I?

You may think that when an athlete sits on the bench, it means he is not good enough to play. Sometimes this is true, but often it is not. For many years, I sat on the bench even though I knew I could be a top NFL quarterback. People said I had the bad luck to be stuck behind a future Hall of Famer, Joe Montana. But the way I saw it, I had an opportunity to learn from the best. When I finally got my chance, I decided it was time to show what I had learned. My name is Steve Young, and this is my story . . . "

"When I finally got my chance, I decided it was time to show what I had learned."

Growing Up

When Steve Young was just six or seven years old, he was already the most popular boy in his neighborhood. Actually, it was Steve's house that was popular—it was the only house on the block with a basketball hoop and the only one with a yard big enough for a football game! There always seemed to be a lot of kids and a lot of games around his house. Even though Steve was younger and smaller than most of the other kids, he liked to be right in the middle of things.

When Steve was eight, his family moved from Salt Lake City, Utah, to Greenwich, Connecticut. He was sad about leaving his friends and a little scared of going to a new school. But Steve met two boys named Kelly and Ed, and soon the three of them did everything together.

Steve was a very fast runner. He played quarterback and running back for Easton Junior High School, and in two years, his team never lost a game. But Steve wanted to do more than

At Greenwich High, Steve excelled in several sports, including basketball (right).

just run. When he entered Greenwich High School, he decided to try out for quarterback on the football team. He made the junior varsity team, but he found that being a quarterback was harder than he had thought. His team lost almost every game, and in one contest Steve threw seven interceptions!

Steve eventually became a good passer by learning from his mistakes and relying on his natural ability. He was such a good athlete that he was named the captain of the school's basketball and baseball teams. He also pitched and played left field for the baseball team, batting .400 and throwing two no-hitters. But Steve's football skills were the most impressive. During his last two years of high school, he was one of the best quarterbacks in the state. In his senior year, he led his team to the county championship game.

Steve comes from a big family. He has three younger brothers—Jimmy, Mike, and Tom—and a younger sister named Melissa. Steve's mother, Sherry, was a teacher. His father, LeGrande, was an attorney for a mining company. His job required him to arrange the details of business deals that involved millions of dollars. Steve looked up to his dad, who had played football for Brigham Young University years before Steve was born. LeGrande's teammates nicknamed him "Grit" because he never gave up. No one was surprised when

The Youngs: Tom, Mike, Grit, Sherry, Jim, Steve, and Melissa

Steve (left) and
younger brother Tom

Steve followed in his father's footsteps and accepted a football scholarship from Brigham Young . . . and years later became an attorney himself!

"My favorite team was the New York Giants. They actually played in Connecticut for a couple of years while their new stadium was being built in New Jersey. My favorite player was Roger Staubach, the quarterback for the Dallas Cowboys. He used to kill the Giants–I think he beat them 11 times in a row from 1974 to 1979! I had posters of Roger all over my room, and I read every story on him that I could find. As it turned out, we would have a lot in common. He had to wait until he was 27 to get a chance to play every day, and I had to wait until I was 29. Also, he was called 'Roger the Dodger' for his running ability, and running is one of my best weapons."

Steve Young loved school. His favorite subjects were history and science. In these subjects, it seemed that there was no limit to what he could learn. Steve always tried to get a desk right up in the front of the classroom, and he raised his hand whenever he had a question. He was not afraid to ask a "dumb" question—as he saw it, asking about something he did not know made it a "smart" question! Steve especially liked when his teacher divided the class into teams and the children competed in spelling and math games.

As Steve got better at sports and joined more teams, he had little time to do his homework and study

A trip to the Hula Bowl

for tests. His parents supported his athletic career, but they were very strict when it came to his studies. Steve's grades came first. If they began to drop, he would not be allowed to play anymore. There were times when his sports and schoolwork took up so much time that he was not able to hang out with his friends. He sometimes wondered if he was making the right decision. Years later, Steve realized that he did. To this day, he is amazed at how often he uses skills he learned in school that he never thought he would need as an adult.

A Kodak All-American

"I loved reading. I always loved books and magazines, and I read them as often as I could. Reading is really the most important thing you can learn in your life. Think about it. Just about everything you do involves being able to read something. You just can't get away from it. As for school, the best approach is to always try to learn as much as you can. Don't limit yourself to certain subjects because those are the ones you think will be important when you grow up. You'd be surprised . . . the more you learn, the easier life is when you get older."

College

Steve Young went to college in the fall of 1980. When he arrived on the campus of Brigham Young University in Utah, he got the shock of his life. He would not be the team's star, nor would he even be a starter. In fact, he was the number-eight quarterback on the team! To make matters worse, one of the coaches seemed to go out of his way to be mean to Steve and often embarrassed him in front of his teammates. Another coach suggested that he consider switching his position to safety. Steve got the message. The coaches did not intend to use him as a quarterback for Brigham Young.

Steve was never more miserable. Between football practice and his studies, he was working more than 14 hours every day. He missed his friends and family back in Connecticut. After the season ended, Steve flew home and told his dad that he was fed

up with football. He was not enjoying himself, and he wanted to quit. "Son," Grit told Steve, "you can quit . . . but you can't come home. I don't live with quitters."

Steve returned to school, and in the spring he got his first big break. A new coaching staff was hired by the university to guide the football team. Ted Tollner, the quarterback coach, took Steve under his wing. Coach Tollner began grooming Steve to replace starter Jim McMahon, who would graduate at the end of the 1981 season. Steve got into a few games and played well, securing his spot as the Brigham Young starter in 1982.

At BYU, Steve passed for more than 7,000 yards and threw 56 touchdown passes.

Jim McMahon as a Chicago Bear

Steve had a nice year in 1982, but did not perform as well as McMahon had the previous season. Critics questioned whether he was getting special treatment because he was related to school founder Brigham Young and he was a Mormon. Young answered the doubters the following season by leading the team to a 10–1 record. He completed more passes for more yards than any quarterback in the country. He led everyone with a completion percentage of 71.3. That means 7 of every 10 passes he threw were caught!

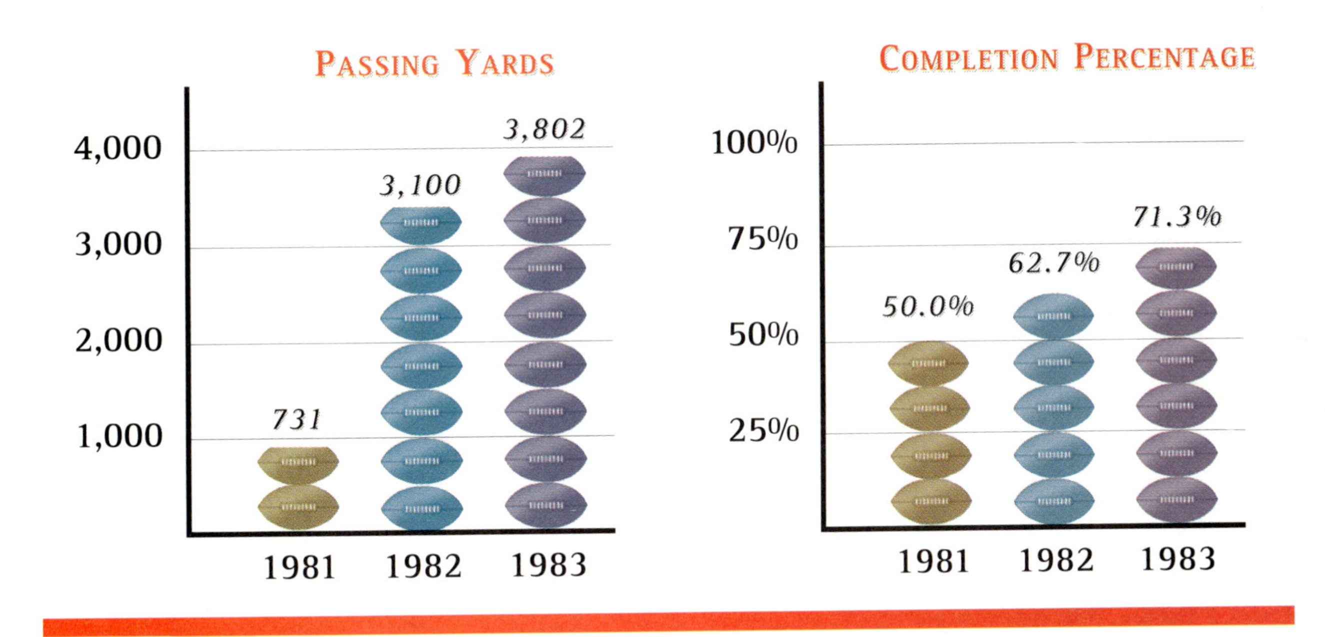

Steve finished second in the Heisman Trophy voting for the best college player, and was named to the All-America team. "I also was honored as an Academic All-American, which was just as important to me and my family as any of the many awards I won that season."

It was not a coincidence that Steve Young went to Brigham Young University. Brigham Young, who was an important leader of the Mormon Church in the 1800s, was Steve's great-great-great-grandfather. Steve majored in two subjects during his four years in college–international relations and finance. Despite his heavy athletic schedule, he maintained an A average and graduated on time.

Road to the

When Steve graduated from college in 1984, he had two choices. He could fulfill a lifelong dream and play in the National Football League (NFL), or take a chance on the new United States Football League (USFL). There were several advantages to accepting an offer from the USFL. Steve would be guaranteed a starting role with a team in a big city like New York, Los Angeles, or Chicago. He would also make a lot of money if the league was a success.

Steve as a Tampa Bay Buccaneer

If he chose the NFL, he would probably spend two or three years on the bench, but he could probably look forward to a long career. It was a complicated decision. Which would you have chosen?

Super Bowl

Steve chose to play with the new league. He signed a $40-million contract to play for the Los Angeles Express. But two seasons later, the USFL went out of business. Steve received only a small portion of the money that had been promised to him. To make matters worse, he was claimed by the Tampa Bay Buccaneers, one of the worst teams in the NFL!

After setting records at BYU, Steve chose to play in the USFL. He eventually joined the NFL Tampa Bay Bucs.

Steve joined the San Francisco 49ers in 1987.

Steve did his best to play well, but he could not win games all by himself. He was so unhappy playing for losing teams that he asked to be traded. In 1987, the Bucs were willing to listen to any offers for Steve. The San Francisco 49ers happened to be in the market for a backup quarterback. Their superstar, Joe Montana, had suffered a serious back injury the year before, and team coach Bill Walsh suggested to Steve that Montana might soon retire. Tampa Bay, having found a willing taker, completed the deal to trade Steve to the 'Niners.

Incredibly, Montana not only rebounded from his injury, but for the next four seasons, he played some of the best football anyone had ever seen. Poor Steve was stuck on the bench again! Only when Montana missed the entire 1991 season with an elbow injury did Steve get his chance. This would be his shot at proving he belonged in the pros.

Steve responded to this challenge with an excellent year, finishing as the NFL's highest-rated quarterback. His next three seasons were even better. Steve led the league in touchdown passes three times and was named NFL Player of the Year in 1992 and 1994. In those three seasons—1992, 1993, and 1994—the 49ers won 37 of 48 games and were NFC West division champs each season. On January 29, 1995, Steve Young washed away all the years of frustration. He played his best in the biggest game of his career. He passed for a record six touchdowns in Super Bowl XXIX, beating the San Diego Chargers 49-26.

Before he became an All-Pro quarterback, Steve played backup to the great Joe Montana (right).

1980: Returns to Salt Lake City to attend Brigham Young University

1969: Moves from Salt Lake City, Utah, to Greenwich, Connecticut

1984: Signs to play for the Los Angeles Express of the USFL

1985: Claimed by the Tampa Bay Buccaneers

1995: Wins Super Bowl XXIX in Miami, Florida

1987: Traded to the San Francisco 49ers

Game

Eddie Stinnett celebrates his winning touchdown pass to Steve Young.

Steve's biggest play in college came against Missouri—not as a passer but as a receiver. Trailing 17–14 with a few seconds remaining, Young took the snap and lateraled the ball to running back Eddie Stinnett. While all the Missouri players chased Stinnett, Young ran in the opposite direction and Stinnett turned and fired the ball back to him. Young caught it, put a move on one last defender, and rumbled into the end zone for the winning touchdown! No one in the stadium that day could remember seeing a more exciting play.

Action!

Steve started wearing jersey number 8 in junior high school. He was so skinny that his coach said a wider, two-digit number would look silly on him. Steve has worn number 8 ever since.

Steve gets congratulations and respect from team owner Eddie Debartolo, Jr., after winning the Super Bowl.

I think being looked upon as a team leader is something that I've become quite proud of. It is important to gain the respect of your teammates."

Steve's running ability makes him the NFL's ultimate weapon. Not only can he burn a defense with his passing, but he can pick up big yards in the open field if he is forced to run. Some say he could have been an All-Pro running back had he not made it as a quarterback.

Beating the Dallas Cowboys in the 1994 NFC Championship Game was my most satisfying win, because Dallas had beaten the 49ers in the previous two years and had denied us a shot at the Super Bowl."

Dealing

Imagine how frustrating it would be to know you are better than almost everyone else in your sport, except the player in front of you." Steve spent a total of four years as football's best-paid backup, while Joe Montana led the 49ers to triumph in two Super Bowls. Other players might have demanded a trade or said things to make the starter look bad. But Steve knew he could learn a lot by watching, listening, and waiting his turn. In the end, this approach paid off. "A winning attitude will see you through the bad times," he says. "You can learn a lot about yourself fighting through them."

When Steve took over as starting quarterback, he had the pleasure of throwing to All-Pro receiver Jerry Rice (left).

Joe Montana

The Grind

You would never know it by watching him play, but Steve Young did not have a strong arm when he became a college quarterback. In high school, Steve directed an offense that emphasized the running game, and his arm was below average. By lifting weights, stretching, and throwing a football in every spare moment, Steve eventually developed the arm strength he needed to become a big-time quarterback.

Steve's arm strength is no longer in doubt.

The demand for an athlete's time is constant. Here, Steve does an interview after the Super Bowl.

Steve Young has found that the toughest part of being a sports star is having to say No. "Trying to please everybody is impossible," he says. "I get a lot of requests for autographs, and although I want to sign for everybody, sometimes I can't–there's just not enough time. I feel terrible when people go away mad."

NFL linebackers love when a slow-footed quarterback tucks the ball under his arm and decides to run. But they hate seeing Steve Young running. When Steve heads down the field, he attacks defenses with the speed and power of a starting fullback. It's not unusual for him to gain 10 or 20 yards in a carry. If you are a quarterback and like to run, you can use a trick Steve has worked to perfection. By keeping his arm cocked when he breaks out of the pocket, he "freezes" the defense by making opponents believe he might throw the ball just before he crosses the line of scrimmage. If defenders believe he is going to pass, they will not leave their men uncovered. They stay downfield, allowing Steve room to build up a full head of steam before they start closing in.

There will be no pass this time as Steve tucks the ball under his arm and breaks upfield.

The pass is still an option even as Steve eludes the defense.

He Do It?

Family

Steve Young remains close to his brothers, his sister, and his parents, who still live in the same house where he grew up. Steve is not married. Most of the time, he just hangs around with his "second family"—49er teammates Brent Jones and Harris Barton. Or he plays golf and skis with his friends.

Steve doesn't yet have a family of his own, but he can often be found with members of the Young clan. Here he visits with his mother, Sherry, and his niece, Taryn.

Steve thinks of several teammates as close as family. One good friend is Harris Barton (right).

Steve's dad was Brigham Young University's best runner in 1959, leading the team with 423 yards.

Steve shares an October 11 birthday with his brother Mike. Steve was born in 1961, and Mike was born exactly two years later.

A month after Steve signed his $40-million deal with the Los Angeles Express, his five-year-old brother Jimmy won an Easter egg decorating contest. The prize was a $5 bill. "Wow," he said to his mother, "I'm as rich as Steve now!"

What do football people say about Steve Young?

"He was always a hustler and always worked hard at what he was doing."

–Frank Parelli,
Steve's high-school football coach

"Steve Young has great physical ability, an excellent arm, tremendous foot speed, and running ability."

–Mike Holmgren,
Green Bay Packers coach

"Sure there's been pressure on Steve . . . and he's become a darn good quarterback."

–George Seifert, 49ers head coach

"He's the most accurate passer I've ever seen."

–Gil Brandt, former Dallas Cowboys executive

"He can make a great play out of something that shouldn't be a play at all."

–Mike Shanahan,
Denver Broncos head coach

"He's no longer just a great athlete playing quarterback . . . he's a great quarterback."

–Steve Wallace, 49ers tackle

Career

Steve won the Davey O'Brien Award as the country's top college quarterback in 1983. He finished second to running back Mike Rozier in the Heisman Trophy voting.

On Dec 22, 1990, Steve ran for over 100 yards in a game against the New Orleans Saints.

January 29th, 1995. Steve had the greatest day of any quarterback in Super Bowl history, tossing six touchdown passes. It was the first time in his life he had thrown that many—even in backyard games. Steve was not only the Super Bowl XXIX's leading passer, he also had more rushing yards than anyone on either team! He was voted MVP.

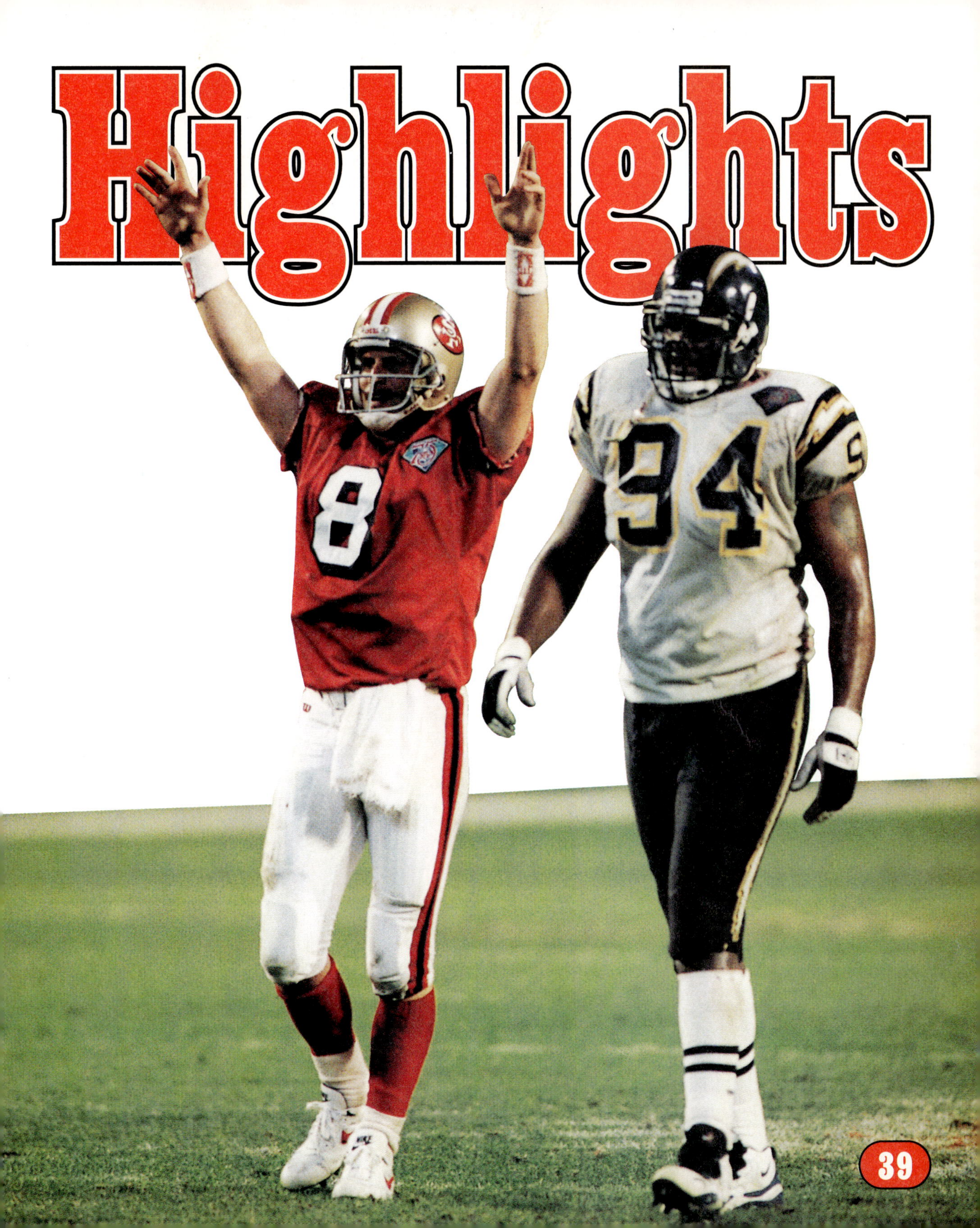
Highlights
8
94

SF
56

Steve has completed a higher percentage of passes than any quarterback in NFL history.

Steve was the NFL Player of the Year in 1992 and 1994, leading the league in passing percentage and touchdowns each season.

Steve's 112.8 quarterback rating in 1994 is the highest mark in football history.

Reaching

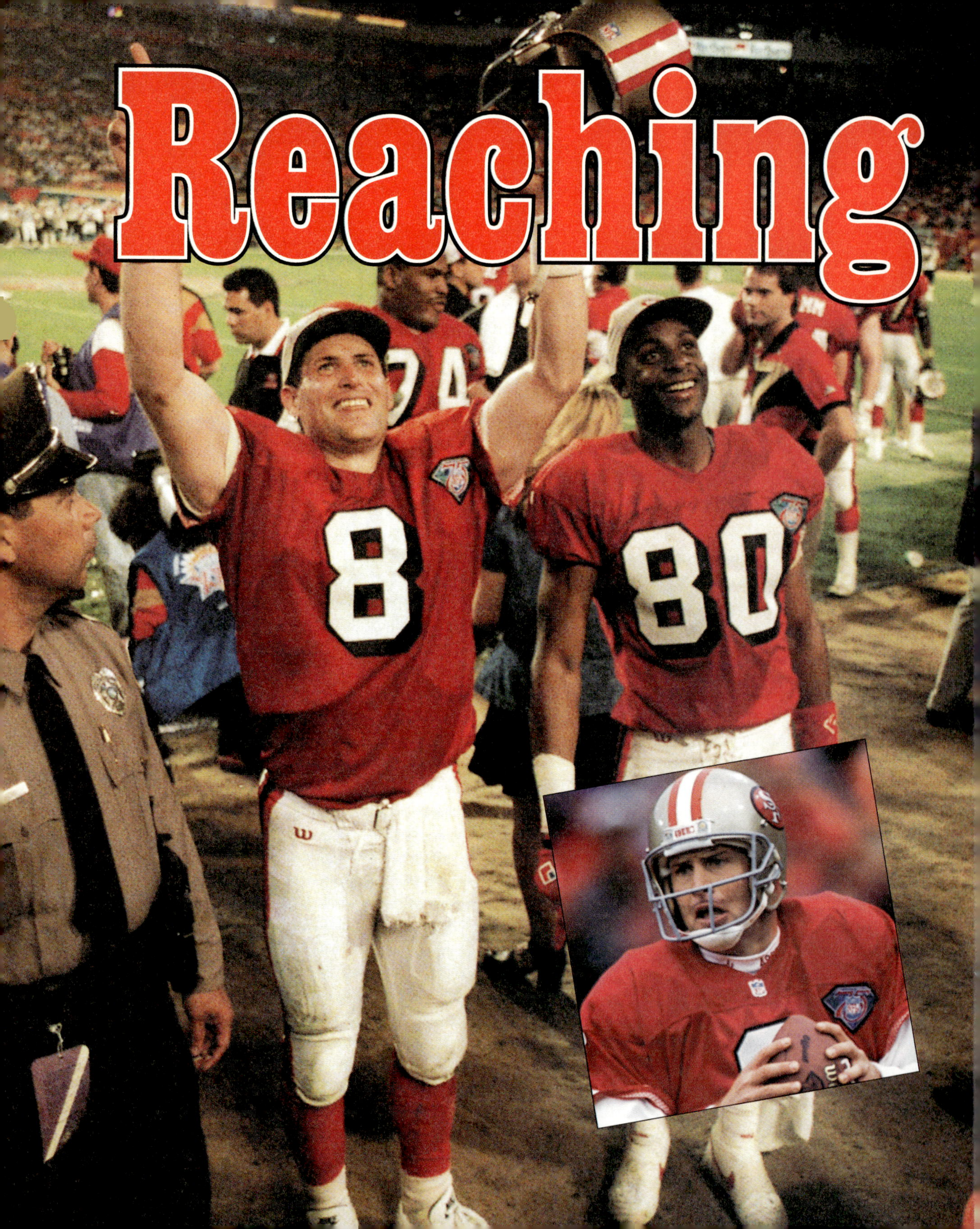

Steve Young might be pro football's most generous player off the field. Steve started the Forever Young Foundation in 1993 to raise money for organizations that encourage the development, security, and strength of the family. He regularly rolls up his sleeves and joins his volunteers in fund-raising events, including two golf tournaments, art auctions, and special football clinics.

Name: Jon Steven Young

Born: October 11, 1961

Height: 6' 2"

Weight: 205 pounds

Uniform Number: 8

College: Brigham Young University

Steve is one of the NFL's few left-handed quarterbacks. He is also the only player in history to lead the NFL in quarterback rating four years in a row. In addition to Steve's 176 passing touchdowns, he has scored 36 rushing touchdowns in his pro career.

Year	Team (League)	Games	Attempts	Completions	Yards	Pct.	TD Passes	QB Rating
1984	Los Angeles Express (USFL)	12	310	179	2,361	57.7	10	80.6
1985	Los Angeles Express (USFL)	13	250	137	1,741	54.8	6	63.1
1985	Tampa Bay Buccaneers (NFL)	5	138	72	935	52.2	3	56.9
1986	Tampa Bay Buccaneers (NFL)	14	363	195	2,282	53.7	8	65.5
1987	San Francisco 49ers (NFL)	8	69	37	570	53.6	10	120.8
1988	San Francisco 49ers (NFL)	11	101	54	680	53.5	3	72.2
1989	San Francisco 49ers (NFL)	10	92	64	1,001	69.6	8	120.8
1990	San Francisco 49ers (NFL)	6	62	38	427	61.3	2	92.6
1991	San Francisco 49ers (NFL)	11	279	180	2,517	64.5	17	101.8*
1992	San Francisco 49ers (NFL)	16	402	268	3,465	66.7*	25*	107.0*
1993	San Francisco 49ers (NFL)	16	462	314	4,023	68.0	29*	101.5*
1994	San Francisco 49ers (NFL)	16	461	324	3,969	70.3*	35	112.8*
1995	San Francisco 49ers (NFL)	11	447	299	3,200	66.9	20	92.3
Totals		149	3,436	2,161	27,171	62.9	176	96.1

*Led League

I am proud of what I have accomplished in my life, both on and off the field. But sometimes I think back to my first year at Brigham Young and wonder what might have happened had I been one of the other guys competing for the quarterback job—one of the guys who didn't make it to the pros. The courses I took in international relations and finance prepared me to move into a number of different careers. I could have worked for a bank, gotten a job with the government or possibly gone into politics. As things turned out, I was lucky enough to have a successful football career. Still, I went back and got my law degree, so I can look forward to practicing law when my playing days are over."

Glossary

ACADEMIC concerning education and learning abilities

ACCURATE exact; correct

ADVANTAGE something that is helpful or useful

APPROACH the steps toward accomplishing a goal

COINCIDENCE an event that happens by chance

COMPLICATED hard to understand

CRITIC a person who finds fault or who doubts

EXECUTIVE someone holding a high position in a company

FINANCE the study of how people, businesses, and countries manage their money

FOUNDER one who starts up a country, business, or college

GROOMING preparing someone to do a job

HUSTLER an energetic, aggressive player

IMPRESSIVE awesome; great

IN THE MARKET shopping; searching

INTERNATIONAL RELATIONS the study of how different countries get along with each other

MAJOR in college, the career you study for is called your *major*

REBOUND bounce back; recover

REQUIRED called for; needed

RETIRE to stop working at a job

SECURE make safe and sure; lock in

ULTIMATE the greatest; the best

Index

About The Author

Mark Stewart grew up in New York City in the 1960s and 1970s–when the Mets, Jets, and Knicks all had championship teams. As a child, Mark read everything about sports he could lay his hands on. Today, he is one of the busiest sportswriters around. Since 1990, he has written close to 500 sports stories for kids, including profiles on more than 200 athletes, past and present. A graduate of Duke University, Mark served as senior editor of *Racquet*, a national tennis magazine, and was managing editor of *Super News*, a sporting goods industry newspaper. He is the author of every Grolier All-Pro Biography.